Cocoa Bean
to
Chocolate

by Rachel Grack

BELLWETHER MEDIA · MINNEAPOLIS, MN

Note to Librarians, Teachers, and Parents:

Blastoff! Readers are carefully developed by literacy experts and combine standards-based content with developmentally appropriate text.

Level 1 provides the most support through repetition of high-frequency words, light text, predictable sentence patterns, and strong visual support.

Level 2 offers early readers a bit more challenge through varied simple sentences, increased text load, and less repetition of high-frequency words.

Level 3 advances early-fluent readers toward fluency through increased text and concept load, less reliance on visuals, longer sentences, and more literary language.

Level 4 builds reading stamina by providing more text per page, increased use of punctuation, greater variation in sentence patterns, and increasingly challenging vocabulary.

Level 5 encourages children to move from "learning to read" to "reading to learn" by providing even more text, varied writing styles, and less familiar topics.

Whichever book is right for your reader, Blastoff! Readers are the perfect books to build confidence and encourage a love of reading that will last a lifetime!

This edition first published in 2020 by Bellwether Media, Inc.

No part of this publication may be reproduced in whole or in part without written permission of the publisher. For information regarding permission, write to Bellwether Media, Inc., Attention: Permissions Department, 6012 Blue Circle Drive, Minnetonka, MN 55343.

Library of Congress Cataloging-in-Publication Data

Names: Koestler-Grack, Rachel A., 1973- author.
Title: Cocoa bean to Chocolate / by Rachel Grack.
Description: Minneapolis, MN : Bellwether Media, Inc., 2020. | Series: Blastoff! readers. Beginning to end |
  Includes bibliographical references and index. | Audience: Ages 5-8. | Audience: Grades K-1. |
  Summary: "Relevant images match informative text in this introduction to how chocolate is made.
  Intended for students in kindergarten through third grade"– Provided by publisher.
Identifiers: LCCN 2019027416 (print) | LCCN 2019027417 (ebook) |
  ISBN 9781644871386 (library binding) | ISBN 9781618918086 (ebook)
Subjects: LCSH: Cocoa processing–Juvenile literature. |
  Chocolate candy–Juvenile literature. | Cacao–Juvenile literature.
Classification: LCC TP640 .K64 2020 (print) | LCC TP640 (ebook) | DDC 663/.92–dc23
LC record available at https://lccn.loc.gov/2019027416
LC ebook record available at https://lccn.loc.gov/2019027417

Editor: Rebecca Sabelko   Designer: Laura Sowers

Printed in the United States of America, North Mankato, MN.

Table of Contents

Cacao Tree	4
From Tree to Factory	6
Time to Make Chocolate!	10
Chocolaty Treats!	20
Glossary	22
To Learn More	23
Index	24

Cacao Tree

Did you know chocolate comes from trees?

Where Do Cocoa Beans Grow?

N
W · E
S

The Ivory Coast produces 1.8 million tons (1.6 million metric tons) of cocoa beans each year.

Cacao trees grow in **tropical** countries. Their fruit pods hold cocoa beans. These beans become chocolate!

From Tree to Factory

cocoa beans and pulp

cacao pod

Farmers **harvest** ripe cacao pods. They take out the cocoa beans and **pulp**.

The beans **ferment** for up to a week. Flavors start to form!

fermenting beans

Farmers dry the beans
in the sun. They rake the
beans to dry them evenly.

Ivory Coast Tree Loss

7 out of 10 trees lost to make room for cocoa farming

The dried beans are shipped to chocolate makers!

Chocolate makers **roast** the cocoa beans. Each maker decides how long and hot the beans are roasted.

This creates different flavors and dries the shells.

Winnowing breaks the shells away from the cocoa **nibs**.

Wheels roll the nibs through a **grinder** to make **cocoa mass**.

cocoa mass

Making Chocolate: Grinding and Conching

grinding

conching

winnowing cocoa beans

Chocolate makers add sugar, milk powder, or flavors. They stir the cocoa mass for hours or days.

conching chocolate

Longer **conching** makes finer chocolate!

The chocolate is slowly
tempered. Then nuts or
candy pieces can be added.
Tempering helps the chocolate
harden into smooth and crisp bars.

Cocoa Bean to Chocolate

1

harvest cacao pods and
remove cocoa beans and pulp

2

ferment and
dry beans

3

roast beans

4

winnow shells
and grind nibs

5

conch chocolate mass and
temper melted chocolate

6

mold chocolate
and eat!

Chocolate makers pour the melted chocolate into **molds**. It hardens as it cools.

Finally, the chocolate is ready to eat!

Chocolaty Treats!

Think of all the chocolate goodies. You find it in candy, cookies, and cake. It comes as frosting and fudge.

Nothing makes a yummy
treat like chocolate!

Glossary

cocoa mass—pure chocolate paste

conching—heating and stirring cocoa mass to bring out its flavors

ferment—to let something age; a chemical change takes place during fermentation.

grinder—a machine that crushes beans to powder

harvest—to gather crops

molds—empty containers used to shape liquids into solids

nibs—pieces of cocoa beans that have been roasted and dried

pulp—the soft, juicy part of fruits and vegetables

roast—to cook something in a hot oven

tempered—slowly heated and cooled

tropical—relating to the tropics, a hot region near the equator

winnowing—breaking off the cocoa bean shells and blowing away the broken bits

To Learn More

AT THE LIBRARY

Fretland VanVoorst, Jenny. *Chocolate: How Is It Made?* Minneapolis, Minn.: Jump!, 2017.

Heos, Bridget. *From Cocoa Beans to Chocolate.* Mankato, Minn.: Amicus, 2018.

Ridley, Sarah. *Beans to Chocolate.* New York, N.Y.: Crabtree Publishing, 2018.

ON THE WEB

FACTSURFER

Factsurfer.com gives you a safe, fun way to find more information.

1. Go to www.factsurfer.com.

2. Enter "cocoa bean to chocolate" into the search box and click 🔍.

3. Select your book cover to see a list of related web sites.

Index

cake, 20
candy, 16, 20
cocoa mass, 12, 14
conching, 13, 15
cookies, 20
dry, 8, 9, 11
farmers, 6, 8
ferment, 7
flavors, 7, 11, 14
frosting, 20
fudge, 20
grinder, 12, 13
harvest, 6
making chocolate, 13
milk powder, 14
molds, 18
nibs, 12
nuts, 16
pods, 5, 6
pulp, 6
rake, 8

roast, 10
shells, 11, 12
steps, 17
sugar, 14
sun, 8
tempered, 16
tree loss, 9
trees, 4, 5, 9
where cocoa beans
    grow, 5
winnowing, 12, 13

The images in this book are reproduced through the courtesy of: baibaz, front cover (chocolate); Snowbelle, front cover (beans); timquo, p. 3; freedomnaruk, pp. 4-5; Kaiskynet Studio, pp. 6-7, 17 (1); Nabilah Khalil, p. 7; Lucy Brown - loca4motion, pp. 8-9; mavo, pp. 10-11, 17 (3); Jiri Hera, p. 11 (top); Olga Popova, p. 11 (bottom); Max4e Photo, p. 12; LORENVU/SIPA/ AP Images, pp. 12-13; Alejo Miranda, pp. 13 (left), 17 (4); fjmolina, pp. 13 (right), 15; Cultura Creative (RF)/ Alamy, pp. 14-15; Oleksii Bilyk, pp. 16, 17 (5); stephanie. brand, p. 17 (2); dem10, pp. 17 (6), 18-19; Martin Novak, p. 19; tlindsayg, pp. 20-21; Rawpixel.com, p. 21; M. Unal Ozmen, p. 23.